Fourth Step Workbook

AA Journal For Alcohol Recovery

Diana Lea

FOURTH STEP WORKBOOK: AN AA JOURNAL FOR ALCOHOL RECOVERY by DIANA LEA

Copyright © 2022 by DIANA LEA
Published by IMAGINATE PUBLISHING.

First Printing, 2022

First Edition 2022

ISBN: 9798428044584

Disclaimer: The information contained in this book is for informational and educational purposes only and should not be used as a substitute for professional medical advice, diagnosis, or treatment. If you have a healthcare issue, including addiction, it is recommended that you consult with a licensed professional or healthcare provider.

Disclaimer: Every reasonable effort has been made to ensure that the information provided in this book was correct at the time of publication. The author and publisher do not assume and hereby disclaim any responsibility and/or liability for any loss, damage, disruption, or adverse effects resulting from the use of the information found within this book, whether by errors, omissions, negligence, accident, or any other cause.

Books published by Imaginate Publishing are available at special discount rates for bulk purchases by corporations, institutions, and other organizations. For more information, please contact Imaginate Publishing at info@imaginateonline.com

A sober body does not a make a sober mind.
It is the sober mind which creates a sober body.

– Diana Lea

Contents

Beginning Step Four

We should be sure that we have a sponsor and have already done steps one, two, and three before embarking on step four. This workbook is intended to be worked on with a qualified sponsor, recovery specialist, or addict counselor. It will be all too easy to spiral into self-loathing, completely defeating our recovery, if step four is worked alone. We're going to need someone in our corner for this, we're going deep diving!

And just to be clear, a qualified sponsor is someone who has taken ALL 12 steps as laid out in the *Alcoholics Anonymous* Big Book. If we have chosen to work this step with a qualified sponsor, we need to be sure that he or she is present and leading us through. This is one of the reasons we have sponsors. If there is anything that we are unsure of, we do not hesitate to ask our sponsor. Of course, we might want to prepare for some long talks!

The step four personal inventory is about searching for our grosser handicaps. This will then become part of a life-long process. Once we get to step 10, we'll see that our objectives are to keep our "house clean and in order", correcting our mistakes as they occur. Through this, most of us grow in understanding and effectiveness. Understanding of ourselves, our instincts, our personal impulses, and what really drives us. We will use steps 10 and 11 on a daily basis to look at our "Assets and Liabilities" which will then give us a wonderful "Design for Living" that we'll use to "Recreate our lives" anew.

As diligently as we might work this fourth step, there will be things that we will forget or otherwise feel like we should have included but didn't. We have lived a thousand lives; it would be impossible to remember all of it at once. As long as we are honest and thorough in the working of step four to the best of our ability, as we move through the other steps, there will be time to revisit this one, and will become the norm. We simply use the step 10 inventories to circle back here while using them in our every day.

Now then, let us first understand the language that we will be using else we might feel offended or worthless, which we are not. We are quite valuable albeit fallible.

"Putting out of our minds the wrongs others had done, we resolutely looked for our own mistakes. Where had we been selfish, dishonest, self-seeking, and frightened?"

What do we mean by selfish, dishonest, self-seeking, or frightened?

SELFISH	DISHONEST
Not seeing others point of view, problems or needs	Not seeing or admitting where I was at fault
Wanting things my way	Having a superior attitude–thinking I'm better
Wanting special treatment	
Wanting others to meet my needs–dependence	Blaming others for my problems
Wanting what others have	Not admitting I've done the same thing
Wanting to control–dominance	Not expressing feelings or ideas
Thinking I'm better–grandiosity	Not being clear about motives
Wanting to be the best	Lying, cheating, stealing
Thinking others are jealous	Hiding reality–not facing facts
Wanting others to be like me	Stubbornly holding on to inaccurate beliefs
Being miserly, possessive	
Wanting more than my share	Breaking rules
Reacting from self-loathing, self-righteousness	Lying to myself
Too concerned about me	Exaggerating, minimalizing
Not trying to be a friend	Setting myself up to be "wronged"
Wanting to look good or be liked	Expecting others to be what they are not
Concerned only with my needs	Being perfectionistic
Self-centered, egotistical - "It's about me!"	

SELF SEEKING

Manipulating others to do my will
Putting others down internally or externally to build me up
Engaging in character assassination
Acting superior
Acting to fill a void
Engaging in gluttony or lusting at the expense of another person
Ignoring others' needs
Trying to control others
Getting revenge when I don't get what I want
Holding a resentment
Acting to make me feel good

FRIGHTENED (OF)

Peoples' opinions
Rejection, abandonment
Loneliness
Physical injury, abuse
Not being able to control or change someone
My inferiority, inadequacy
Criticism
Expressing ideas or feelings
Getting trapped
Exposure, embarrassment

We tended to react to people, situations, institutions, and principles the way we did because there was some part of ourself that was either threatened, hurt, or otherwise interfered with. For most of us, these parts we sought to defend and keep safe are our self-esteem, our pride, our financial security, our personal relationships, our ambitions, our emotional security, and our sexual relationships. These are the seven parts that we reacted to:

THE SEVEN PARTS OF SELF DEFINED

- Self Esteem - How I think of myself
- Pride - How I think others view me
- Financial Security - Basic desire for money, property, possessions, etc.
- Personal Relationships - Our relationships with other people
- Ambition - Our goals, plans and designs for the future
- Emotional Security - General sense of personal well being
- Sex Relationships - Basic drive for sexual intimacy

Now let's breakdown our ambitions which are our goals and plans for the future, things that we want. We have these four types:

- Emotional ambitions. Our goals and plans for emotional security. Our "feelings".
- Material ambitions - Our goals and plans for physical and financial security.
- Social ambitions - Our goals and plans towards what people think about us.
- Sexual ambitions - Refers to goals and plans for sex relationships.

We all begin our recovery journey with a boatload of pent-up shame, guilt, and unresolved pain that we have stockpiled over the years. Who wants to deal with all that shit? But now, to find true sobriety, thus truly live, we need to let go of all that stored up garbage. However, we can only do that if we know what it is and where it lies. This is what step four seeks to do. It helps us to find and work through the war zones of our past so that we are no longer at their mercy.

Through the processes of step 4, we get to find out who we really are, and what we really are not. It's not just about finding our defects of character; the well-designed method also helps us to discover our assets as well. And we learn that our problems began long before we ever had our first drink. We may have felt isolated, anxious, depressed, or insecure, and it was our want and drive to change those feelings which led to our drinking.

Alcoholism, addiction, is a disease. We are no more responsible for being an alcoholic than someone with diabetes is for being diabetic. But now that we know we have a disease, like the diabetic, we are responsible for our recovery. We can no longer use our many excuses because we now realize that to keep from dying spiritually, emotionally, and physically we must live the principles of the steps each and every day. We use the steps every day of our lives to move us from discontentment, restlessness, and irritability toward lasting sobriety with serenity and peace of mind.

The lists ahead are long but remember that we are not only looking at people but situations, institutions, and principles as well. As we are working through the lists ahead, we keep on the lookout for paralysis from fear and/or perfectionism. First of all, there is no way anyone can do this work perfectly. Secondly, doing this work doesn't *cause* injury to us but, rather, will *heal* our injuries, including the ones we never even knew we had. And it can be frightening to look at our demons and own them. Demons are pretty damn scary! If we do feel paralyzed at any point, we go ahead and step back and take a deep breath. Then, we look to our sponsor or counselor to guide us, personally, as to what we should do.

Notes or questions for my sponsor and responses:

_____

_____

_____

_____

_____

_____

_____

_____

_____

_____

_____

_____

_____

_____

_____

_____

_____

_____

_____

_____

_____

_____

_____

_____

_____

_____

_____

_____

Making Our Grudge List

It's clear that a life full of resentment leads only to chaos and misery. To the degree that we allow that bitterness in our lives, we waste our time which might have otherwise been filled with joy and peace. For an alcoholic, or any addict for that matter, this is substantially worse. For us, such feelings will almost always guarantee a return to the insanity of alcohol and we drink again. And for us, "to drink is to die". If we hope to really live, we have to face and release our anger.

Realize that the people who wronged us were probably sick as well. Although maybe a different kind of sick from an alcoholic but sick nonetheless. We might not like their symptoms and how they affected us, but other people we have injured don't like ours. We ask our Higher Power to help us show them the same tolerance and patience that we would hope to receive with our symptoms. When someone offends us, we say, "This person is sick, how can I help? God of my understanding keep me from getting angry but instead let your will be done." We won't be able to help everyone, but at least we can have tolerant view of them.

We need to take our time and be honest here. This will be an ongoing task throughout our recovery as we remember more. We go through our life, our whole life. We must be brutally honest and completely thorough.

The first list we will make is our grudge list. In the first column, we list the people, circumstances, institutions, or principles that angered us. We give the reason(s) they angered us in the second column. In the third column, we will identify what it is/was about it that threatened us. Usually, we find that our self-esteem, emotional security, finances, ambitions, personal relationships, or sexual relationships were either threatened, hurt, or otherwise interfered with.

After we make our grudge list on the first of the two-page spread, we will look at it from an entirely different perspective using the second. Without a new view, the wrong-doing of others, whether real or not, might actually have the power to kill. We cannot wish our anger away any more than alcohol.

SE - Self-Esteem	AB - Ambitions
PD - Pride	PR - Personal Relations
EM - Emotional Security	SX - Sex Relations
FS – Financial Security	

Using the key above, here is an example of what our first grudge list page should look like:

I resent:	Because:	It affects My:
Mr. Brown	His attention to my wife.	SX, SE
Mr. Brown	Told my wife about my affair.	SX, EM
Mr. Brown	Brown may get my job at the office.	FS, PD
Mrs. Jones	She committed her husband for drinking. He is my friend.	PR, SE, EM
My employer	Threatens to fire me for drinking and padding my account.	SE, FS, AB
My wife	Misunderstands and nags.	PD, PR, SE
My wife	Likes Mr. Brown.	SX, EM, SE
My wife	Wants house put in her name.	FS

We look at our list again but now we're looking for *our* mistakes. We need to be painfully honest with ourselves here. Where were we selfish, dishonest, anxious (frightened), or self-seeking? Although "a situation had not been entirely our fault," we still need to see where *we* went wrong.

SF - Selfish
DH - Dishonest
FR - Frightened
SS - Self-seeking

Using the key above, here is an example of what our second grudge list page should look like:

What's my part?	Was I:
I didn't give my wife the attention she needs.	SF, SS
Cheating on my wife was hurtful and wrong.	DH, SS
I hate to admit, I'm not as honest as Brown and he has better judgement than I do.	DH, FR
I kept my friend out late many times so I would have someone to drink with.	SF
I didn't always stay sober the entire work day and I wasn't honest in my account.	DH, SS
I usually didn't do what I told my wife I would do.	DH, SF
I didn't give my wife much of my time.	SF
Being an alcoholic, I didn't provide my wife with much security.	FR, SS

Questions for my sponsor and responses:

_____

_____

_____

_____

_____

_____

_____

_____

_____

_____

_____

_____

_____

_____

_____

_____

_____

_____

_____

_____

_____

_____

SE - Self-Esteem   AB - Ambitions
PD - Pride   PR - Personal Relations
EM - Emotional Security   SX - Sex Relations
FS – Financial Security

I resent:	Because:	It affects My:

SF - Selfish
DH - Dishonest
FR - Frightened
SS - Self-seeking

What's my part?	Was I:

7

SE - Self-Esteem   AB - Ambitions
PD - Pride   PR - Personal Relations
EM - Emotional Security   SX - Sex Relations
FS – Financial Security

I resent:	Because:	It affects My:

SF - Selfish
DH - Dishonest
FR - Frightened
SS - Self-seeking

What's my part?	Was I:

SE - Self-Esteem   AB - Ambitions
PD - Pride   PR - Personal Relations
EM - Emotional Security   SX - Sex Relations
FS – Financial Security

I resent:	Because:	It affects My:

SF - Selfish
DH - Dishonest
FR - Frightened
SS - Self-seeking

What's my part?	Was I:

SE - Self-Esteem   AB - Ambitions
PD - Pride   PR - Personal Relations
EM - Emotional Security   SX - Sex Relations
FS – Financial Security

I resent:	Because:	It affects My:

SF - Selfish
DH - Dishonest
FR - Frightened
SS - Self-seeking

What's my part?	Was I:

Notes/Responses/Reactions

Making Our Fear List

From the 4th edition of the AA Big Book Page 67-68

This short word [fear] somehow touches about every aspect of our lives. It was an evil and corroding thread; the fabric of our existence was shot through with it. It set in motion trains of circumstances which brought us misfortune we felt we didn't deserve. But did not we, ourselves, set the ball rolling? Sometimes we think fear ought to be classed with stealing. It seems to cause more trouble.

We reviewed our fears thoroughly. We put them on paper, even though we had no resentment in connection with them. We asked ourselves why we had them. Wasn't it because self-reliance failed us? Self-reliance was good as far as it went, but it didn't go far enough. Some of us once had great self-confidence, but it didn't fully solve the fear problem, or any other. When it made us cocky, it was worse.

Relying on ourselves, with all our self-confidence, to run our own show never fully resolved our fears or any other real problem. In fact, our self-confidence only made us cocky which made matters worse. We miserably failed as the rulers of our universe. But now we no longer have to fear any mistake we make because we now trust the flawless, infinite Higher Power rather than our imperfect, finite selves.

Now it's time to review our fears thoroughly. We list all the things that we are afraid of including things we are afraid of losing. We must remember to include the fears that have no connection to our resentments. Why do we have them? Here is an example of what a fear list should look like:

SE - Self-Esteem
PD - Pride
EM - Emotional Security
FS – Financial Security

AB - Ambitions
PR - Personal Relations
SX - Sex Relations

Using the key above, here is an example

What I fear:	Why?	It affects My:
Losing my wife	I love her but I don't feel worthy	SE, ES, SX
Losing my job	I like it need it but I don't feel good enough	SE, FS, AB
Failing	I feel like a loser	SE, PD, AB
Losing my friends	People won't like me if they really knew me	EM, PR

Here are some prompting questions derived from the 12 'n 12 book to help get you started:

What sex situations have caused me anxiety, bitterness, frustration, or depression?
What work situations have caused me anxiety, bitterness, frustration, or depression?
What financial situations have caused me anxiety, bitterness, frustration, or depression?
What home situations have caused me anxiety, bitterness, frustration, or depression?
What situations in society have caused me anxiety, bitterness, frustration, or depression?
Did I have fear and insecurity about my ability to do my job?
Did I have fear and insecurity in regards to my marriage?
Did I have fear and insecurity in regards to my children?
Did I have fear and insecurity about my financial situation?
What things or people am I afraid of losing?
What phobias do I have?
What institutions or principles cause me anxiety?

Questions for my sponsor and responses:

SE - Self-Esteem   EM - Emotional Security   AB - Ambitions
PD - Pride   FS – Financial Security   PR - Personal Relations
                                                    SX - Sex Relations

What I fear:	Why?	It affects My:

SE - Self-Esteem   EM - Emotional Security   AB - Ambitions
PD - Pride   FS – Financial Security   PR - Personal Relations
   SX - Sex Relations

What I fear:	Why?	It affects My:

SE - Self-Esteem   EM - Emotional Security   AB - Ambitions
PD - Pride   FS – Financial Security   PR - Personal Relations
                                               SX - Sex Relations

What I fear:	Why?	It affects My:

Making Our Sexual Conduct List

From the 4th edition of the AA Big Book Page 68-70

We reviewed our own [sexual] conduct over the years past. Where had we been selfish, dishonest, or inconsiderate? Whom had we hurt? Did we unjustifiably arouse jealousy, suspicion, or bitterness? Where were we at fault? What should we have done instead? We got this all down on paper and looked at it.

A few new terms and a few terms geared towards this inventory list:

SELFISH
- Using another to meet my needs (sex, approval, attention, mothering/fathering)
- Not seeing needs or problems of other
- Wanting to look good or be liked
- Taking my feelings out on other
- Wanting to control other
- Wanting special treatment/taken care of
- Wanting more than I gave
- Not being a friend

DISHONEST (to me or others)
- Not being clear about my motives (wanting sex, approval, attention, mothering/fathering, etc.)
- Leading someone on
- Being ambiguous
- Saying I care more than I do
- Not admitting my sexual orientation
- Being perfectionistic
- Thinking I'm better (grandiosity)
- Cheating on other

INCONSIDERATE
- To other, family, friends, coworkers, etc.
- Putting others or myself at risk of disease, legal involvement, and embarrassment

JEALOUSY
- Of other, family, friends, coworkers, etc.
- How did I cause jealousy (deceiving, flirting, ambiguous, etc.)?

SUSPICION
- Of other, family, friends, coworkers, etc.
- How did I cause suspicion (lying, flirting, being vague, coming home late, etc.)?

BITTERNESS
- About other, family, friends, coworkers, etc.
- About me (guilt, shame)
- How did I cause bitterness?

Like the grudge list, we take our time and be honest here. This too will be an ongoing task throughout our recovery as we remember more. We go through our life, our whole life. We must be brutally honest and completely thorough.

In the first column, we list the people, circumstances, institutions, or principles that we hurt with our sexual conduct including innuendoes and comments. We record what it was that we did, didn't do, said, or didn't say in the second column. In the third column, we will identify what feelings were unduly aroused, either for us or the other, by our conduct or words.

After we make our sexual conduct list on the first of the two-page spread, we will look at it from a different perspective using the second.

JL - Jealousy
SP - Suspicion
BT – Bitterness

Using the key above, here is an example of what our first sexual conduct page should look like:

Who did I hurt?	What did I do?	Unduly:
My wife	I had an affair on my wife.	JL, BT
My mistress	I seduced her into an adulterous affair. I didn't tell her I was married.	SP, BT

We look at our list again but now we're looking for what we should have done. We need to be painfully honest with ourselves here. Where were we inconsiderate, selfish, dishonest, anxious (frightened), or self-seeking?

IN – Inconsiderate   FR - Frightened
SF - Selfish   SS - Self-seeking
DH - Dishonest

Using the key, here is an example of what our second sexual conduct page should look like:

Was I:	What I should have done:
IN, DH, SS	I should have remained faithful to my wife.
SF, DH, SS	I should have been honest and told her that I was married.

Here are some prompting questions from the 12 'n 12 book to help get you started:

Who was hurt and how badly?
Appraising each situation fairly, can I see where I have been at fault?
When did my selfish pursuit of the sex relation damage other people and me?
How did my selfish pursuit of the sex relation damage other people and me?
In just what instances did my selfish pursuit of the sex relation damage other people and me?
Did I ruin my marriage and injure my children?
Did I jeopardize my standing in the community?
Just how did I react to these situations at the time?
Did I burn with a guilt that nothing could extinguish?
Did I insist that I was the pursued and not the pursuer and thus absolve myself?
How have I reacted to frustration in sexual matters?
When denied, did I become vengeful or depressed?
When denied, did I take it out on other people?
If there was rejection or coldness at home, did I use this as a reason for promiscuity?
What sex situations have caused me anxiety, bitterness, frustration, or depression?
Did these perplexities beset me because of selfishness or unreasonable demands?
If my disturbance seemed to be caused by others, why can't I accept what I can't change?
Did fear and insecurity about my sexuality kill my confidence and fill me with conflict?
Did I try to cover up feelings of inadequacy by evading responsibility, faking, cheating, or lying?
Did I overvalue myself?
To what extent have my own mistakes fed my gnawing anxieties?

Questions for my sponsor and responses:

JL - Jealousy
SP - Suspicion
BT – Bitterness

Who did I hurt?	What did I do?	Unduly:

IN – Inconsiderate   FR - Frightened
SF - Selfish   SS - Self-seeking
DH - Dishonest

Was I:	What I should have done:

JL - Jealousy
SP - Suspicion
BT – Bitterness

Who did I hurt?	What did I do?	Unduly:

IN – Inconsiderate   FR - Frightened
SF - Selfish   SS - Self-seeking
DH - Dishonest

Was I:	What I should have done:

IN – Inconsiderate   FR - Frightened
SF - Selfish   SS - Self-seeking

JL - Jealousy
SP - Suspicion
BT – Bitterness

Who did I hurt?	What did I do?	Unduly:

IN – Inconsiderate   FR - Frightened
SF - Selfish   SS - Self-seeking
DH - Dishonest

Was I:	What I should have done:

Making Our "Harm to Others" List

Like the grudge and sexual conduct lists, we take our time and be honest here. This too will be an ongoing task throughout our recovery as we remember more. We go through our life, our whole life. We must be brutally honest and completely thorough.

In the first column, we list the people, circumstances, institutions, or principles that we hurt with our behavior, words, or lack thereof. We record what it was that we did, didn't do, said, or didn't say in the second column. In the third column, we will identify where the behavior came from. Were we being selfish, self-seeking, dishonest, anxious (frightened), inconsiderate, playing God?

After we make a list of those we hurt and how on the first of the two-page spread, we will look at it from a different perspective using the second.

SF – Selfish
SS - Self-seeking
DH - Dishonest
FR – Frightened

IN – Inconsiderate
LC – Lack of self-control
GD – Playing God

Using the key above, here is an example of what our first hurt list page should look like:

Who I hurt:	What I did:	I was:
Mr. Brown	I ended our friendship for telling my wife of my affair.	SF, FR,
Mr. Brown	I treated him coldly at the office.	FR, IN
Mrs. Jones	I called her names and gossiped about her.	LC, GD, FR
My employer	I drank on the job and padded my account.	LC, DH, SS

We look at our list again but now we're looking for what we should have done. We need to be painfully honest with ourselves here. We also identify where we were at fault. Were we using our self-will, self-reliance, self-pity? Were we motivated by material security, our self-esteem, our pride, personal relationships, our ambitions, sexual relationships, financial security, or emotional security?

WL - Self-will
RL - Self-reliance
PT - Self-pity
SE - Self-esteem

PD - Pride
MS - Material Security
FS - Financial Security
EM - Emotional Security

PS - Personal Relationship
SX - Sexual Relationship
AB - Ambitions

Using the key, here is an example of what our second hurt list page should look like:

Where was I at fault?	What I should have done:
SP, SR, ES	I should have thanked Brown for respecting my wife.
SR, PR, AB, FS	I should have treated him with respect at the office.
SP, SE, PS, ES	I should have offered to help Mrs. Jones with her husband.
SW, FS	I shouldn't drink at work and I should be honest in my accounts.

Here are some prompting questions from the 12 'n 12 book to help get you started:

Who was hurt and how badly?
Did I ruin my marriage and injure my children?
When denied what I wanted, did I become vengeful or depressed?
When denied what I wanted, did I take it out on other people?
Did I try to cover up feelings of inadequacy by evading responsibility, faking, cheating, or lying?
Did I try to cover up feelings of inadequacy by complaining that others failed to recognize my truly exceptional abilities?

Did I have such unprincipled ambition that I double-crossed and undercut my associates?
Was I extravagant?
Did I recklessly borrow money, caring little whether I repaid it or not?
Was I too cheap, refusing to support my family properly?
Did I cut corners financially?
Did I try to cover up my spending by juggle charge accounts?
Did I find funds to drink by manipulating the grocery budget?
Where was I financially wasteful?

Questions for my sponsor and responses:

_____

_____

_____

_____

_____

_____

_____

_____

_____

_____

_____

_____

_____

_____

_____

_____

_____

_____

_____

_____

_____

_____

_____

_____

_____

_____

_____

_____

SF – Selfish   IN – Inconsiderate
SS - Self-seeking   LC – Lack of self-control
DH - Dishonest   GD – Playing God
FR – Frightened

Who I hurt:	What I did:	I was:

WL - Self-will   PD - Pride   PS - Personal Relationship
RL - Self-reliance   MS - Material Security SX - Sexual Relationship
PT - Self-pity   FS - Financial Security AB - Ambitions
SE - Self-esteem   EM - Emotional Security

Where was I at fault?	What I should have done:

SF – Selfish
SS - Self-seeking
DH - Dishonest
FR – Frightened

IN – Inconsiderate
LC – Lack of self-control
GD – Playing God

Who I hurt:	What I did:	I was:

WL - Self-will   PD - Pride   PS - Personal Relationship
RL - Self-reliance   MS - Material Security SX - Sexual Relationship
PT - Self-pity   FS - Financial Security AB - Ambitions
SE - Self-esteem   EM - Emotional Security

Where was I at fault?	What I should have done:

SF – Selfish
SS - Self-seeking
DH - Dishonest
FR – Frightened

IN – Inconsiderate
LC – Lack of self-control
GD – Playing God

Who I hurt:	What I did:	I was:

SF – Selfish
SS - Self-seeking
DH - Dishonest

IN – Inconsiderate
LC – Lack of self-control
GD – Playing God

WL - Self-will	PD - Pride	PS - Personal Relationship
RL - Self-reliance	MS - Material Security	SX - Sexual Relationship
PT - Self-pity	FS - Financial Security	AB - Ambitions
SE - Self-esteem	EM - Emotional Security	

Where was I at fault?	What I should have done:

SF – Selfish   IN – Inconsiderate
SS - Self-seeking   LC – Lack of self-control
DH - Dishonest   GD – Playing God
FR – Frightened

Who I hurt:	What I did:	I was:

WL - Self-will	PD - Pride	PS - Personal Relationship
RL - Self-reliance	MS - Material Security	SX - Sexual Relationship
PT - Self-pity	FS - Financial Security	AB - Ambitions
SE - Self-esteem	EM - Emotional Security	

Where was I at fault?	What I should have done:

Making Our Respect List

Although we have acted quite disrespectful much of the time, it doesn't mean that we don't *feel* respect. It just means that we didn't really know how to *show* our respect. Therefore, some of those on this list are probably on one or more lists of those we hurt or were resentful towards. This is something we alcoholics tend to do; we mistreat those we respect and care for.

Who/what I respect:	Why I respect this person, institution, principle:

Who/what I respect:	Why I respect this person, institution, principle:

Who/what I respect:	Why I respect this person, institution, principle:
Who/what I respect:	Why I respect this person, institution, principle:

Who/what I respect:	Why I respect this person, institution, principle:
Who/what I respect:	Why I respect this person, institution, principle:

Making Our Poor Decisions List

Science has shown that alcoholics have irregularities in the areas of the brain connected to emotional and cognitive processing and control – our decision making. Since alcoholism affects the part of the brain that helps us to think clearly and rationally, our decision-making and rational thinking abilities go straight out the window. Through long-term use, it becomes harder to work out what we are feeling and makes us less likely to be able to really think through any potential consequences. Hence, our bad decisions.

The good news is that through abstinence, we can regain control over these areas of our brain. The longer we go without alcohol, the more of our brain, and our mind, we get back and the more control we really have over our life.

In the first column, we list our poor decisions. We list the people, circumstances, institutions, or principles that angered us. In the second column, we will identify which part(s) of self we were relying on. Usually, we see that we were relying on our self-control, our will, relying on ourself, or falling into the pity trap.

After we make our poor decisions list on the first of the two-page spread, we will look at it from an entirely different perspective using the second.

LC – Lack of self-control	RL - Self-reliance
WL - Self-will	PT - Self-pity

Using the key above, here is an example of what our first grudge list page should look like:

A Poor decision I made:	Motivation:
I got angry with my boss for passing me over for a promotion and quit my job.	LC, PT
I cheated on my wife after she called me an alcoholic.	RL, WL, PT

We look at our list again but now we're looking for what we should have done. We also identify where we were at fault. We need to be painfully honest with ourselves here. Were we self-seeking, dishonest, or anxious (frightened)? Were we motivated by material security, our self-esteem, our pride, personal relationships, our ambitions, our sexual relationships, our financial security, or emotional security?

SS - Self-seeking	PD - Pride	PS - Personal Relationship
DH - Dishonest	MS - Material Security	SX - Sexual Relationship
FR – Frightened	FS - Financial Security	AB - Ambitions
SE - Self-esteem	EM - Emotional Security	

Using the key above, here is an example of what our second grudge list page should look like:

Where was I at fault?	What I should have done:
FR, PD, AB, FS	I should have found another job before quitting the one I had.
DH, SE, PR, SX, EM	Realized my wife was telling me that she was hurt y my drinking.

Questions for my sponsor and responses:

_____

_____

_____

_____

Questions for my sponsor and responses:

LC – Lack of self-control
WL - Self-will
RL - Self-reliance
PT - Self-pity

A Poor decision I made:	Motivation:

SS - Self-seeking   PD - Pride   PS - Personal Relationship
DH - Dishonest   MS - Material Security   SX - Sexual Relationship
FR – Frightened   FS - Financial Security   AB - Ambitions
SE - Self-esteem   EM - Emotional Security

Where was I at fault?	What I should have done:

LC – Lack of self-control
WL - Self-will
RL - Self-reliance
PT - Self-pity

A Poor decision I made:	Motivation:

SS - Self-seeking   PD - Pride   PS - Personal Relationship
DH - Dishonest   MS - Material Security   SX - Sexual Relationship
FR – Frightened   FS - Financial Security   AB - Ambitions
SE - Self-esteem   EM - Emotional Security

Where was I at fault?	What I should have done:

SS - Self-seeking   PD - Pride   PS - Personal Relationship
DH - Dishonest   MS - Material Security   SX - Sexual Relationship
FR – Frightened   FS - Financial Security   AB - Ambitions
SE - Self-esteem   EM - Emotional Security

LC – Lack of self-control
WL - Self-will
RL - Self-reliance
PT - Self-pity

A Poor decision I made:	Motivation:

SS - Self-seeking PD - Pride PS - Personal Relationship
DH - Dishonest MS - Material Security SX - Sexual Relationship
FR – Frightened FS - Financial Security AB - Ambitions
SE - Self-esteem EM - Emotional Security

Where was I at fault?	What I should have done:

SS - Self-seeking PD - Pride PS - Personal Relationship
DH - Dishonest MS - Material Security SX - Sexual Relationship
FR – Frightened FS - Financial Security AB - Ambitions
SE - Self-esteem EM - Emotional Security

LC – Lack of self-control
WL - Self-will
RL - Self-reliance
PT - Self-pity

A Poor decision I made:	Motivation:

SS - Self-seeking   PD - Pride   PS - Personal Relationship
DH - Dishonest   MS - Material Security   SX - Sexual Relationship
FR – Frightened   FS - Financial Security   AB - Ambitions
SE - Self-esteem   EM - Emotional Security

Where was I at fault?	What I should have done:

SS - Self-seeking   PD - Pride   PS - Personal Relationship
DH - Dishonest   MS - Material Security   SX - Sexual Relationship
FR – Frightened   FS - Financial Security

Making Our Good Decisions List

I do think it important to also see where we might have gone right in our life. We alcoholics didn't always make poor choices, we made a few good ones sometimes too. We should recognize our strengths so we can build upon those now and in the future.

A good decision I made:	Why it was good:

A good decision I made:	Why it was good:
A good decision I made:	Why it was good:

A good decision I made:	Why it was good:
A good decision I made:	Why it was good:

Making Our Character Flaws List

Part of our journey is learning our misconceptions and how those have injured us, our relationships, our dreams, our potential. Not to mention steal our joy and, more importantly, our peace. Getting that back, or for the first time, is a painful road but one worth traveling. It begins with self-acceptance. Accepting all our parts-good, bad, and boring. To do that, we have to *SEE* those parts. Those things that we have disowned, denied, hidden out of our sight.

How do we do this? One flaw at a time. It's going to be painful; it's going to be scary; we're going to struggle with guilt, we're going to fight the good fight with denial. If, while we are doing an inventory of our shit, we deny a character flaw, we can be sure it belongs to us. We are human, we have flaws. But we can't begin to correct any of them until we come into full acceptance of them. We must be careful as we work this list and never forget that we are more than our flaws. Remember and accept your humanness.

Remember that we are not seeking to recover *FROM* anything, we're seeking to recover (get back) that which we have lost, or, never got the chance to cultivate and develop in the first place. Like feeling good enough and fully accepted and loved *IN SPITE OF* our shortcomings rather than because of our good qualities.

It is possible to have a particular character flaw as well as it's opposite, a character asset. Usually, it depends on the person or circumstances as to which aspect of our character comes out. I mention this only because   some of us get stuck on assuming that if we possess a particular flaw or asset, it means all the time, no matter what, which isn't true.

Questions for my sponsor and responses:

_____

_____

_____

_____

_____

_____

_____

_____

_____

_____

_____

_____

_____

_____

_____

_____

_____

_____

_____

_____

Character Flaws

Afraid	gossiping	resisting growth
aggressive	grandiose	rude
angry	greedy	sarcastic
anxious	hateful	self-centered
apathetic	hostile	self-defeating
apprehensive	hypersensitive	self-destructive
argumentative	hypocritical	self-hating
arrogant	ill-tempered	self-important
avoidant	impatient	self-indulgent
belligerent	inconsiderate	self-justifying
bitchy	indecisive	self-pitying
bitter	indifferent	self-righteous
blocking	indolent	self-seeking
boastful	insecure	selfish
careless	insincere	shy
cheating	insolent	slob/sloppy
closed	intolerant	slothful (lazy)
competitive	irresponsible	spiteful
compulsive	isolating	stealing
conceited	jealous	stubborn
contemptuous	judgmental	sullen
contradictory	lack of purpose	superior
controlling	lazy	superstitious
cowardly	loud	suspicious
critical	lustful	tense
crude	lying	thinking negatively
cynical	malicious	timid
deceitful	manipulative	treacherous
defensive	masked	undisciplined
defiant	mean	unfair
denying	morose	unfaithful
dependent	nagging	unfriendly
destructive	narrow minded	ungrateful
dishonest	obscene	unkind
disloyal	oppositional	unrealistic
disobedient	over emotional	unreliable
disrespectful	perfectionistic	unsupportive of others
enabling	pessimistic	untrustworthy
envying	poor hygiene	useless
evasive	possessive	vain
exaggerating	prejudiced	verbose
falsely modest	pretentious	vindictive
falsely prideful	procrastinates	violent
fantasizing	projecting (negative)	vulgar
fearful	rationalizing	wasteful
forgetful	reckless	willful
gluttonous	resentful	withdrawn

And any other dysfunctional ways of acting, feeling, or thinking which cause me or others pain.

Making Our Character Assets List

W̲e alcoholics aren't all bad all the time. We do have feelings including feelings for other people, institutions, and principles. As a reminder, I repeat the following:

It is possible to have a particular character flaw as well as it's opposite, a character asset. Usually, it depends on the person or circumstances as to which aspect of our character comes out. I mention this only because some of us get stuck on assuming that if we possess a particular flaw or asset, it means all the time, no matter what, which isn't true.

Now we make a list of the good characteristics we have.

Character Assets		
accepting	faithful	praising
accepting of the inevitable	firm	purposeful
accepts help but is self-reliant	flexible	quiet
acts promptly	forgiving	realistic
admiring	frank	realistic goals
admitting wrongs	free	reasonable
agreeable	friendly	reliable
alert	generous	respectful
altruistic	gentle	responsible
being positive	good self-esteem	reverent
brave	good-natured	secure
broadminded	good-tempered	self-accepting
calm	grateful	self-confident
candid	guileless	self-fulfilling
careful	healthy sexuality	self-restrained
caring	helpful	selfless
caring of others	honest	serene
cheerful	honestly earns	setting boundaries
clean	hopeful	sharing
clear sighted	humble	sincere
closed-mouth	industrious	sociable
concerned	interested	straightforward
concerned for others	intuitive	succinct
concerned with others	kind	supportive
confidant	let it go, esp. of other's lives	taking action
conscientious	loving	tasteful
considerate	loyal	thankful
considered actions	moderate	thoughtful
consistent	modest	thrifty
cooperative	non-controlling	tolerant
courageous	non-judgmental	trusting
courteous	obedient	trustworthy
decisive	open minded	unassuming
disciplined	open to criticism	understanding
doesn't personalize	optimistic	vulnerable
emotionally stable	outgoing	willing
empathetic	patient	willing to grow
faces problems and acts	polite	
fair	practical	

And any other functional ways of acting, feeling, or thinking which does not cause me or others pain.

My Asset:	How can I expand on this?

My Asset:	How can I expand on this?

My Asset:	How can I expand on this?

Making Our Moral Inventory

Now that we have outlined most of our bullshit, we write out our moral inventory. This too will be an ongoing list as our eyes become more opened through our recovery.

Here is an example of a moral inventory list:

I lie to the people I care about, and it's hurt them.

I bring others down with my self-loathing and shame.

I boast about my achievements.

I am judgmental of others.

I have alienated those around me by my selfishness.

I have taken my anger out on my family and friends.

Here are some prompting questions derived from the 12 'n 12 book to help get you started:

Do I jeopardize my standing in the community?
When denied, do I become vengeful or depressed?
When denied, do I take it out on other people?
If there is rejection or coldness at home, do I use this as a reason for promiscuity?
Do fear and insecurity kill my confidence and fill me with conflict?
Do I try to cover up feelings of inadequacy by evading responsibility, faking, cheating, or lying?
Do I try to cover up feelings of inadequacy by complaining that others fail to see my truly exceptional abilities?
Do I overvalue myself and play the big shot?
Do I have such unprincipled ambition that I double-cross and undercut others?
Am I extravagant?
Do I recklessly borrow money, caring little whether I repaid it or not?
Am I too cheap, refusing to support my family properly?
Do I cut corners financially?
Do I try to cover up my spending by juggle charge accounts?
Do I find funds to drink by manipulating the grocery budget?
Am I financially wasteful?

My Moral Inventory:

My Moral Inventory:

My Moral Inventory:

My Moral Inventory:

Memorizing the Serenity Prayer

We know the mess we made of our lives by living according to our own will. Or what we believed in the moment was our will. Our lack of insight and wisdom became clear. What would happen, then, if we lived according to the will of something greater? Something more wise than we?

When we live for a purpose greater than ourselves, not only do we have something to believe in, we also have a reason to wake up, to pray, to dream, to work towards that dream, and to stay sober. We have a reason to love life even when things aren't going so well.

We know that we have already failed miserably. We failed ourselves and our loved ones. We failed God if there is one. But as long as we breathe, we have the opportunity to change the outcome. Our outcome and that of our life.

From the 4th edition of the AA Big Book Page 70-71

If we have been thorough about our personal inventory, we have written down a lot. We have listed and analyzed our resentments. We have begun to comprehend their futility and their fatality. We have commenced to see their terrible destructiveness. We have begun to learn tolerance, patience, and good will toward all men, even our enemies, for we look on them as sick people. We have listed the people we have hurt by our conduct, and are willing to straighten out the past if we can.

In this book you read again and again that faith did for us what we could not do for ourselves. We hope you are convinced now that God [of your understanding] can remove whatever self-will has blocked you off from Him. If you have already made a decision, and an inventory of your grosser handicaps, you have made a good beginning. That being so you have swallowed and digested some big chunks of truth about yourself.

We commit the Serenity Prayer to memory if we haven't already. Write out the Serenity Prayer, as many times as there is space to write it, and say it out loud 10 times. Record it on the notepad in your phone. Feel free to replace the name "God" with what you call your Higher Power.

Remember to recite the Serenity Prayer whenever you're emotionally distressed, stressed, indecisive, and anytime you get an urge to drink.

God, grant me the serenity to accept the things I cannot change, the courage to change the things I can, and the wisdom to know the difference. May your will, not mine, be done.

More From Imaginate Publishing

FOR THE BOLD & BRAVE:

AN AA'S LITTLE HANDBOOK Of Hope Prayers Inspiration & Laughs: AA Acronyms, Prayers, Jokes & More

GET THAT FUNKY MONKEY OFF MY BACK! The Smoker's Way To Quit: (A Sweary Kickass Trigger Tracker)

FIVE MINUTE GUIDED TRIGGER TRACKER & BEHAVIOR CHECKER: A Logbook For Alcoholics And Addicts

DIARY OF AN ADDICT: 5 Minute Guided Trigger Tracker Logbook With Daily Journal

AA POWERFUL 12 STEP WORKBOOK With TRIGGER TRACKER & Selfcare Check-Ins

STEPPING THROUGH THE FIRST 90 DAYS: 12 Step Journal With Daily Entries For Steps 10, 11 & 12

FOURTH STEP WORKBOOK: AA Journal For Alcohol Recovery

MAKING OUR 4-COLUMN GRUDGE LIST: A 4th Step Inventory Workbook:

JOURNALING THROUGH THE NEXT SIX MONTHS: 10th Step Journal For Recovering Alcoholics

A BELIEVER'S TOOLBOX:

JOURNEY THROUGH THE BIBLE: A Chronological Bible Reading Plan & Journal: With Scripture Tracker

4-MONTH BIBLE STUDY PLANNER & JOURNAL With Weekly Bible Verse: SOAP Bible Study Journal

52 WEEK BIBLE STUDY PLANNER With Inspirational Quotes From The Bible

BIBLE STUDY JOURNAL: Drawing Closer To God

GRATITUDE JOURNAL With Inspirational Quotes From The Bible

200 PAGE NOTEBOOK With Inspirational Quotes From The Bible

UNDATED PLANNER & BIBLE STUDY JOURNAL: Making Time For God (12 month personal planner)

2023 PLANNER & BIBLE STUDY JOURNAL: Making Time For God

SUCCESS IS PLANNED – PERSONAL PLANNERS:

SUNFLOWERS & BUTTERFLIES UNDATED Monthly & Weekly Planner (12 month personal planner)

2023 PERSONAL PLANNER: Monthly, Weekly & Daily: Purple Floral

THIS IS MY YEAR 2023 PERSONAL PLANNER: Sleek Black

2022-2023 MIDYEAR PLANNER for Academic or Fiscal Planning

2022-2023 ACADEMIC PLANNER FOR COLLEGE STUDENTS: Hourly

2023-2024 MONTHLY PLANNER: 24 Month Planner

2023-2027 FIVE YEAR PERSONAL PLANNER: 60 Month Agenda

JOURNALS FROM IMAGINATE:

MAKING LOVE TO MY DEMONS: SHADOW WORK GUIDED JOURNAL & WORKBOOK: with Prompts

RUSSELL CONWELL'S ACRES OF DIAMONDS and Success Journal

MY BADASS RECIPES: Blank Recipe Book / MY BADASS COCKTAILS: Blank Beverage Recipe Book

ONE LINE A DAY 5 YEAR JOURNAL: The Story Of Me

COMPOSITION NOTEBOOKS:

120 Page Sunflowers & Butterflies College or Wide Ruled

200 Page Christmas Themed College or Wide Ruled

39845767R00051